THE COLOR OF ALL THINGS

MERCER
UNIVERSITY PRESS

Endowed by

TOM WATSON BROWN

and

THE WATSON-BROWN FOUNDATION, INC.

THE COLOR OF ALL THINGS
99 Love Poems

PHILIP LEE WILLIAMS

MERCER UNIVERSITY PRESS | Macon, Georgia
2015

MUP/ P503

Published by Mercer University Press
1501 Mercer University Drive
Macon, Georgia 31207

9 8 7 6 5 4 3 2 1

Books published by Mercer University Press are printed on acid-free paper that meets the requirements of the American National Standard for Information Sciences—Permanence of Paper for Printed Library Materials.

The poem "Our waiter is not coming back," published as "The Waiter," is reprinted by permission of *The Georgia Review.*

ISBN 978-0-88146-523-5
Cataloging-in-Publication Data is available from the Library of Congress

For Linda

Winner of the Adrienne Bond Poetry Award

Past Winners

Seaborn Jones, *Going Farther into the Woods than the Woods Go*
(published 2012)

Kelly Whiddon, *The House Began to Pitch*
(published 2013)

Megan Sexton, *Swift Hour*
(published 2014)

Books by
PHILIP LEE WILLIAMS

NOVELS

Emerson's Brother
The Divine Comics
The Campfire Boys
A Distant Flame
The True and Authentic History of Jenny Dorset
Blue Crystal
Final Heat
Perfect Timing
Slow Dance in Autumn
The Song of Daniel
All the Western Stars
The Heart of a Distant Forest

POETRY

The Color of All Things: 99 Love Poems
The Flower Seeker: An Epic Poem of William Bartram
Elegies for the Water

NONFICTION

It is Written: My Life in Letters
In the Morning: Reflections from First Light
Crossing Wildcat Ridge: A Memoir of Nature and Healing
The Silent Stars Go By

CHAPBOOK

A Gift from Boonie, Seymour, and Dog

THE COLOR OF ALL THINGS

I.

Something luminous in the way you turn back
toward me once to be sure, sunstroked, spring-
fed or gilded, and my own garnet quilt arranged
quite casually, so you may misunderstand us.

Something unexpected in the way you go ahead
and do not ask me to follow you but mark the trail
anyway, as if you planted periwinkle stepstones
into which we grow as we reach to know and know.

I begin to realize a feeling of return in your eyes.
I step back toward you and hear the hum of sun
and cannot see more. There is a path and a door
that stun me toward you, something luminous

in us and yet apart, no matter what love I try.

II.

I will be in the barn if you need me,
raked into the hayloft of our years.

The same mouse lies, finger of a glove,
upon the beam each time I go there,
steadiest of my symbols, staring down.
I imagine it wonders why I stoop now
in the ice-field of my brows, stop, soften
our ticking. The clock of our cow turns
toward milk. I read off the years of breath
on these colder days. And yet you will
not let me shade to ash, not quite yet.

I pause to let my footprints pass me by,
and I say, Not yet, not quite yet.
The field will not take me quite yet.

III.

I ask you for one plowshare shoulder blade,
the one you first turned toward me, so we
may break earth and resurrect our barley days.

Your eyes laugh, but the straight plowed line
of your lips unmoves us. Young wheat, on rising,
looks like grass in the roadside fields, asking

if we have not yet learned the time for harvest.
I ask you for a hand to scythe it, raw sienna
in the hard-won umber of our growing days.

Your cheeks smile, but the puddles go to gleam
with sharper urgency, feeding land we walked
until it went silent as the hay bales in our rain.

I ask you for this possible love before the hull
cracks, and we know for sure. I ask your arms
for wild oats once more, here where the leaves

joyfully wither, drift down to make soil dream
of that slow ripening we grew to hold so plain.
I ask for an hour in that warm and gilded glade.

I ask you for one plowshare shoulder blade.

IV.

What insect should I be? They live on,
have survived a million million years,
so I would be a shifting witness of you,
the summer humming of your breasts,
the sentry louder than cicada howls.

I'm not so much these days for owls
and their presumed sagacity, so I will not
grow you feathers, send you off to glide
beneath the canopy in the hunting night.
Rather, I'll supply the firefly's spark,

pass the code, evade the evening lark
as I crumble, gene to gene, yet go on
with my raptured flight. I would not be
a mammal or a bird to cry your virtues
limb to lamb and back to black again.

I will grow my insect wings and start to sin
and sing against the ruptured hive. Once
more alert, alive to your memorial touch,
I will be the vector of your forest name,
the cricket's crown, the firefly's mane.

V.

You are nothing like glass,
not a pane I could shatter
with a word. A woman
across the street is late
for work, speeds up
the sidewalk cracks until
they slash beneath her
as a jump rope marks
its playground's dust.

She glances over to see
how perfectly slow you
are on our street side,
how unfragile you have
made yourself for me.

I could shout to her
that I am the friable one,
the crumble of our arms,
but surely she must sense
it, know that nothing shall
hammer you into shards
all this life long, that
you hold back what rages
in me, tries to roar downstream
but is held, filling reservoirs,
liquid and lasting
and headed along with you
to break and break and break,
if only I could bend and pass.
You are nothing like glass.

VI.

Between us, we have enough dead loved ones
now that just waving as they pass by takes half
our time. Your mother must have bumped
into mine by now at cards or in the wandering
of their painless days. Your strange uncle stands
out by the tulip poplar tree in our front yard,
toothpick hummed from one side of his mouth
to the other, continuing to say nothing in his nod.

My grandfather is still frozen in a wedding photo
from the early Fifties, the last days before illness
slammed him into bed. I am a decade older now
than he was then, but I wave anyway, hoping he
will recognize in me the shape of our lineage.

I want to believe that you will be the one
to wave me off into the woods of genealogy,
not the other way around, because I watch
the gathering of old witnesses more easily
than you do, for some reason (our finest girl,
my lineal ascendant), in these days upon the sun.

VII.

You were telling me after dinner
about the Brown Mountain Lights,
a phenomenon in North Carolina
that could be ball lightning
or the simple reflection
of luminous patterns
from distant cars or planes.

You told me the Kingston Trio
recorded a song about them
back when we were all
C-G-D and took our comfort there.

You said we need our
mysteries, and just like that
you cocked your head
the way you always do
when you remember
something but cannot
tell me if what lights
you is a song I know
or will know in the world
we shall dance tomorrow.

VIII.

I nearly died before we met,
almost eaten by a shark, of all things,
and by now you have heard the story
of the red foam and dorsal slicing
of that southern sea so many times
you could easily imagine a life
shaped around another man,
not one who let himself be cut
to bits while swimming in sneakers
on the John Pennekamp Coral Reef
State Park, for God's sake.

Your imagined husband might
have been promising, had a father
with a family seat on the stock exchange,
could have bought you a swimming pool
with a house attached. You would
have bronzed your slender body,
cooled down the sun by touching
the can of Falstaff to your neck.

But in your poolside security,
you would have seadreamed-up
a man writing himself back toward
the boat, scribing sonnets of blood
upon the surface of all water,
knowing he could not walk back
to such safety and not minding
that he was close enough to death
that he might be the old, old story
of one pretty girl he'd never met.

IX.

Heaven is not summer's glare to us.
We love a dark cold rainy day by the fire,
reading Austen, cats snug as old age
in our laps. Not Austen, actually—that
was a poetic device I thought might
sound lovely to you, but you aren't
listening to me anyway but reading
a novel about prehistoric women
striking out for unknown lands
to find fire once more. I am reading
a biography of Frank O'Hara but
keep putting it down to challenge
Richard Powers to two-out-of-three
falls. I lose, always, the crowd boos
me, so I retreat to Barton Cottage
and sit by the sputtering fire, add up
the consequences of my inaction.

To my surprise, summer there is
a pleasant time, not what it has become
for Georgia, a ghastly, choking poem
in which prehistoric women decide
to roam not for fire but toward ice,
into the love of cold that freezes us
as lovers who are never healed by heat
for long but held tightly in these flames.

X.

We speak of each other
in the third person sometimes:
She must come to him to share her sorrow
as an old friend has died unexpectedly,
a boy who loved her decades gone.
He will feel the grind of a grudge
against the dead boy (now old, though),
and say to her: I try to be kind about
your past lovers, but I still want
to hit him, challenge him to a war
of syntax and political knowledge
at a party when we are twenty-one.
She lets her eyes narrow with glee;
he could never wreck her old love,
for memories are indestructable
and he, just last week, hurt his knee
while raking leaves to make neat
her sense of him, to believe that he
is stronger than he ever is, ever was,
or ever will be, until he is the unspoken one.

XI.

Our woods are sprayed with rue anemones,
pale rose sepals upcupping the thin sun.
I was going to compare the tuberous,
starchy roots to some aspect of your body
or subcutaneous attraction to me, but,
honestly, it goes down deeper than that.

We are common in rich woods,
our leaflet tips are rounder each year
as those of *Anemonella thalictroides* grow,
and yet this misses our point or at least
one point that grows in me and will until
I lie beneath the murmur of rue anemones.

We are not in our woods or of them.
The hardwoods that trudge down toward
the creek laugh when they hear us coming,
bipedal stalks that blossomed so long ago
that our early, fertile scent has long faded.
So what? We have outlived the hickories

that blew down from straight-line winds
last April, the largest and most majestic
nouns between us and water. And here
in March, the rue anemones once again
pasture the undercanopy, awaken in deadfall,
grin that we still pass by and still believe.

XII.

I love the old photograph of you
pretending to catch a fish, you
in jeans and a crimson coat, you
with the look of a girl surprised, you
learning to love pretense, you
convincing yourself wholly, you
enjoying the flowering of you.

Mirrors attack now—attack me,
I mean, lie in jowls, shade me
so my eyes look comic, the me
of haters and the sneering, me
with shoulders falling down, me
hiding with more passion now, me
the weak impersonator of all me.

But you hold a stick in joy, you
pretend it's a fly-rod, that you
have caught the big one, and you
can't quite believe how bright you
are with your hands, or that you
can feed us with the air-fish, you,
young forever as we both catch you.

XIII.

What I feel for you is slower than
the Amish, more like a black-and-white
photograph of the Amish, not working
to plant or harvest their corn but sitting
on plain benches in their Sunday plainest,
smiles etching up the clear possibility
that in the next week there shall be rain.

I tell you I am going out to hitch up
the team and plow the south hillock
as you kneel to palpate the earthy breasts
of beets, the pubescent cabbages unfolding
secrets we have kept for all our decades.

No—this moment in our lives is too slow
for that. We are more like old undusted
bric-a-brac in a corner cabinet, porcelain
rudders, the objects we took when our
grandparents died, when the family came
to their house and divided up the only things
with value, the last crop that will grow.

I feel like the small donkey with one leg
broken and lost, and you are a shot glass
from Atlantic City, and yet we are slower
than that, slower than a photograph
of the Amish, once cherished but now lost,
black and white, filling us with fertile days.

XIV.

That whole family crying
the day we moved,
that whole family
so mentally and emotionally
naïve others called them
damaged, the ones
whose horse came
to the fence that fall,
and we fed it apples,
fresh, hard fruits
with sun burnished
on the crimson skin,
and the whole family
crying and hugging us
even though we had
only spoken across
the fence for a few
months, unspeaking
our arms, saying without
murmuring it that we
were the only ones
who ever hugged them
on either side
of the fence,
and O God how they
would miss that,
miss us.

XV.

Our waiter is not coming back.
We know at least that much, my love,
that our buttered breadsticks and salad
were a ruse to keep us in the memory
of the wait-staff for all of their lives.
I have given you so little lately,
have given others even less, so this
seems a small gift, to freeze here
in the middle of a ten-times-told
tale of our long lives and offer it
to them. We are both youngly laughing
in the frieze we leave, your face
just over an empty plate, mine
thrown back in Frans Hals hilarity,
wine-flushed and cocked aside.
Our waiter stands at the edge
of the kitchen and studies us,
glad now that we will never age,
will not break our lobster-shell
bones or turn potato pale
as we are wheeled down the hall
into surgery. The others dining out
here have given him little, nothing,
but we have paused forever so he
can see the happiness of those
he comes each night to serve.
I want to give you more each day,
not an epic love with voyages back
from tragedy and all suffering,
but the motion of my hand toward
you as we pass over the street,
nourishment for our solitary crossing.

XVI.

Your sister's friend has died
from complications following surgery,
and I want to grieve but only met him
a few times. The seemly thing is elusive,
isn't it? When I bury my deaf old dog
may I cry without considering
one species cannot ever wear the skin
of another? Should I merely be wistful,
an apple holding on one more day past
the second frost? Evidently we are alone
in the moment of each decision,
so we do not act alone but seem
to crawl toward a consensus,
the millipede uncertainty of love,
as if the sun's brief flare on the glasses
of our grandfathers came back once
and relieved us of the need to know,
much less to be wistful or to grieve.

XVII.

It's raining. Good for me. Outside
my study's windows I can just see
the bare black trunks against
this plum sky as day eases back.
I wonder why funeral directors
never use dark bedding in coffins:
rich crimson, ripe-grape purple,
even a moonless, icy-night black.
I think something is escaping me
more often these early mornings,
the ability to respond to Bartók
with proper delight, a written-out
schedule for grocery shopping
and love. I can't quite see leaves
in their baby albums opening
on the trees, but they're widening,
and soon a canopy cradling bugs
will lie above me. The rain that is
falling fits into this somehow,
the cowl of an unholy spirit
as he wanders away into stone
forever, the inner darkness on
which you may place my roses,
knowing I will not be present
for the resurrection of that sky
which domed us so long ago
that we could mistake the sound
of rain for the tears of old folks,
not sad to be leaving but recalling
their arrival, their misted dawn.

XVIII.

I have placed my reincarnation order:
I wish to return as an Allis-Chalmers Model B
tractor from 1940, nearly all the original
orange paint gone, spindle pins
and drag links missing. There will be
no chance I'll ever start again,
what with my cracked oil sump
and my breather cap two counties over,
being found at this very minute by a boy
with an inexpensive metal detector.

My torque tube will have been removed
in a scrap metal drive for the War.
With my four-cylinder vertical piston engine,
frozen with rust and warpage, you will
easily find me in Bloom's field across
the road. With my ability to produce
over thirteen horsepower on the drawbar,
any lingering doubt you plow up
will turn clod-on-clod into my arms.

Or rather I want to come back
as a Percheron leaning against a tree,
too old to work, swatting flies, looking
with my liquid brown eyes into yours.

Our plowing days are done one afternoon.
But I will be able to carry you back
down to the house at least, where
you can stand on the front porch
with our grandchildren and tell me
goodbye in your Sunday clothes.

XIX.

What if love is no more than
an amino acid, and the responsible gene
is present in some of us and not in others?
What if love is preordained circumstance,
planned from early childhood by the way
a mother laughed at her husband
in the kitchen when he told her a joke
he heard at work that day? What if
the crook of cranes is merely the white
interrogative of a natural urge north,
and my fricatives all indicate
a confidence that evolved out
of my genealogy nine generations back?
What if purring is a cat's treaty
with all wars, those near its paws
or the ones back in its mousing days?
What if love is a nugget of dark chocolate
with almonds—eat one and the world
bursts into song, and she warms her cheek
on yours? What if love is that light
you remember from college that was split
on the hanging glass crystal in the kitchen
window, the one that drew a blue cross
on your T-shirt as you headed out to class?
What if love is the absence of one thing
or another, not the presence of my tendency
to sing when I see your name in a book,
attached to a character that is not you,
speaking to another man who is not me?

XX.

Bulb plants are like Aaron Copland to me,
so predictable, so in need of open affection,
too obvious for repeated bearing. The only
thing I enjoy now is raking leaves. It reveals
what is beneath the burnt sienna of my hands,
my original intentions, things quite possibly
still growing in the tenderest of our flesh.

Yes, an iris is lovely. Sure, jonquils uproam
the thinnest sun. But with bulb plants there
is never the melancholy sense of how death
reduces us to our repetitive howling days.
Each year, there they are, back from vacation
underground, blossoming like small trollops,
then leaving green shoots to stand for them

over weeks and weeks while their flowers
memorialize color and form. We will not
be back after we fall. You know that much.
And each year we do not come back the same
as we were forty seasons past. What, I wonder,
is the point in bringing back the same beauty
over and over and still be warned not to cut

down the green stems—they must fall over
naturally, rot with slow grace, tide the air
as it grows warm then warmer. We were
annuals from our first meeting. Annuals never
know death is final, comes so soon, requires
a flash of violet or buttercream, or presents
us not as we will be, but as we are now, once.

XXI.

You translate me into English.
I want to mean the same thing
the Danes say when they speak
of a quiet morning, of rain,
of that place neither land nor sea,
where we stand in a closing fog
and reach to touch the unseen—
for me, the illusion of you;
for you, the possible me.

XXII.

You are the woman in the moon,
aren't you? Not a man, as night-lit
starers had always seen, but a girl
gleaming down upon the creek
that runs on, not listening to owls
in their proud and fruity songs.
You are the woman in the moon
that lies like a Cherokee rose
just above the pasture out there
beyond us, aren't you? You hum-up
the madrigal geese, and I think
it's just for me, but now that I
reconsider, you probably meant
your iced light for another man,
for a river, an ocean tide, a command
to be fertile and add or multiply.
You are the woman in the moon,
aren't you? Reflecting on me,
my own hovering and love-lit owl.

XXIII.

Drips of rain from the roof
but another noise, the distant engine
of a large sea-going vessel, men asleep
for the most part, and a storm scratching
at the radar's edge. I try to see concern
on the face of this commercial fisherman
who comes inside from a now-lashing rain,
showers dripping from the bill of his cap
as he sits and clears his throat. He can't
quite believe the circular scan, wonders
if he should awaken the others—Bob,
whose wife has left him for a rock drummer,
Ron, whom others call "The Piston"
for his jackhammer relentlessness.

No. I was mistaken. It is the dishwasher
I turned on when I got up then forgot
as I have nearly forgotten your name,
sometimes fear it will never surface
again, and suddenly, like the sun
shimmering through a storm, there
you are, there it is, and there I would be.

XXIV.

I have not yet decided on cremation or embalming,
but this morning I am so sick of my broken body,
my rough and ugly face, that perhaps I could imagine
a way to vanish suddenly when it's time, to let go
of the hand you were not holding very tightly, anyway.
You will look around and my-goodness the room
for a moment and then go on with laundry, games,
or the book due tomorrow at the local library.

I want to be the lover in a romantic comedy, the one
who is an object of amusement, if not derision,
for the first hour, then I come into the focus
our heroine must possess, who suddenly realizes
I am attractive in a deeply soulful way. Then it's
a gorgeous autumn in New York, and the Park
is filled with yellow and ochre leaves, wet lanes,
and our friendship changing into a gentle love.

Maybe cremation would be better because then
this plug-ugly mug would be gone for all time
except for the unfortunate remaining photographs,
and in memory you might begin to think that
you were wrong, that I was handsome in my own way,
that at least I wasn't embalmed so that if some
forensic question arose, and they had to dig me up,
you'd see that I was what I always knew I was,

yearning, reaching, not enough fire to warm you
but not frozen in your heart for all time, either.

XXV.

The plasterer is here. He wants to know
where he should begin, and I say I am
sorry, but I don't believe we have any.
The walls between us are just sheetrock
or castle cracks, hunks of malachite or
hewed sandstone, but mostly words
we speak to hold the distance around
us as solidly as we believe love should
hold us but too often has not, not quite.

I have let him in anyway, the plasterer.
He has already started in the den,
has his trowel out, and is mixing what
he uses to solidify our days, will next
scrape the surface of our easing hours
and will not stop, even if we ask him
to let us fall, to let us lie down in peace.

XXVI.

The horses head up from pasturing.
The Canada geese try singing, fail again.
The skaters head west from Rockefeller Center.
The hands all become lovely swimmers.
The friend waves to you one first time.
The only time I saw you, neurons fired.
The racehorse muscles flexed away from me.
The flight, your elegance, made me ache.
The silver-gray trunks pretend it is winter.
The way you looked when you let me in.
The night fills with horses and geese.
The frozen moon skates on our pond.
The presence of migratory horses wakes
the nature of nerve-endings, enfolds us.
The cats curl by the flame of your hands.
The horses head out to pasturing.

XXVII.

We sit chatting at the table
in the corner, and our waiter
has once more brought us water
but nothing else, stilled water
clear as that river beside
the road north of Franklin,
North Carolina, where ruby
mines wink up their carmine
chips. I pick up my glass
to propose a toast,
but I can't pretend to see
the clear cyan sky
from beneath the river,
my face so close
to the surface you
could tell my intentions,
my truth, with one blush.
We have been here
before, and the menu
always seems different
to you, as if that man
across the water
might improve with time.
I don't know how
to make myself more
than what I fail to be,
so I try to make my eyes
glisten as I stare,
as I recall the words
for you, my eyes too bright
for the diamonds of ice
in your sweating glass.

XXVIII.

A distant thunderstorm begins
to speak with us as the baseball game
rains infield flies. After the third
inning I go on to the porch and see
celebratory lightning bugs as they
fill our woods, calling balls and strikes,
off and on, steal second, suicide squeeze.

Let the games begin, they flash,
go past the fence and catch nothing,
ignore all boundaries. Breathe naturally.
We will awaken with a new game
coming toward us, right into our arms.

XXIX.

You want to stop
and buy honey
at the roadside stand.
Fresh From the Hive,
it says, but the distance
from our first date
makes us Elizabethan actors
when we love, formal,
hive-bound, defending
progeny with duller days.
But it's still golden,
isn't it? The liquid lies
in its waxy comb,
turning the afternoon sun
into a magnifying lass,
there on the shelf
of our roadside stand,
waiting for someone else's
first taste: wild-clover days
and frictionless nights.

XXX.

The reason I lied to you
about touring with Jimi Hendrix
was that I wanted you to like me
in a way that was not possible
for the man who stood there
in front of you like a hubcap
that had rolled in a ditch,
popped from a rust-gone Skylark,
and then been covered
with a flow of red mud,
reduced to remembering
old motions, older maps.
I just wanted you to like me.
No. That's another lie.
I wanted to taste your lips
and to find them as satisfying
as a Nehi Grape Soda after
a Little League game
when I would walk slowly
home, pretending the hit
I did not make won the game
I knew we would always lose.
I am asking you to forgive me.

XXXI.

You are as beautiful
as Nicholas Maw's *La Vita Nuova*,
as rungs on a ladder to heaven,
as a simple, understandable,
explanation of the universe.

What I don't understand
is the emphasis we place
on last words but never
mention last sights,
the vision I have of your
beauty as I fade, going
from fine detail and meaning
to the general outline
of the new life we most often
would not take if we had
a choice. I would choose
lying there, hearing nothing,
forgetting the world I made
in my time, and looking
with a lingering intensity
at your face, my dearest
Beatrice, as I might call you,
smug that for one day
I had won Dante's girl
and would soon be gliding
with you among the deeper
light of the moon and her stars.

XXXII.

Every animal on our acreage
comes silently in the night
to surround us: foxhair, bright
peach-colored bristles, curls
in the amphitheater of birds
and chipmunks. Insects sing
your name. I want them to see
you as I first did, to walk dumb
with stunned light, speaking
your name to each day's weather.

We awaken to raccoon tunes.
Armadillos take off their armor
and stand beneath our window
to applaud. Canada geese which
had already passed us headed
north turn back and settle down
on our lawn, honking happiness,
meaning migration can wait.
Perfect meaning itself can wait.

Mice squeal their counterpoint
to praise your slow waking.
Anoles genuflect on porch rails
and laugh out my human name.
It is not yet light as they gather,
knowing somehow that what
burns in us will cool, the fins
we wear to swim through love
will shed scales and be gone.

I touch your shoulder, and every
pain that life can drape around us
vanishes. The animals are speaking
our names, saying: Come with us
toward the water, into the newest
season of your rusted world.

You may not be here when we return.
Take our wings, crawl away on
a hundred feet, step in fawn-silence
through the woods that slope down
the creek. We can only hold back
the time so long. We can only bring
you this much music one morning
in your brief and climbing lives.

I awaken in the night with bugbites
on my legs, topographic poisons
from my hours raking out the old pen
where we kept dogs long gone to ghosts.
I want to believe human unkindness
cannot destroy our best days, heart
of my lingering light. I want to know
that the dogs are unleashed to roam
this world and wag up new friends.
I take a pen and connect each to each,
the constellation of bites on my thighs,
and try to read in them the route they
took, Thunder and Morgan, old dogs
I resurrect with each scratch and scrape
of the pen. Then I will draw the lines
on back to our own puppy days, when
sun spilled us giggling on our backs
in the grass, when we realized that
everything that had ever been alive
in this world was in motion again,
that there was a time when, falling
into sleep, we did not worry when,
or if, we would waken into free fields
and head toward home or distance,
dancing in the freedom we choose.

XXXIII.

Disliking this poet to his pliable love,
you nudge down the newest butterfly bush
into a water-softened crater you just dug
with your devil's-beard spade. Perennials
cannot twinkle or shout out iambic pentameter,
can they? No. But the Lepidoptera that feed
on buddleja might, from the grim-faced
Death's-head hawk moth bearing its
Acherontia lachesis like a sneeze into May light,
like a glare to all the Noctuidae, and especially
the Gothic moth, whose range can roam across
temperate Eurasia. Have you sold your soul
to grow such lovely plants while I sell mine
to grow wings upon a single word? I want
to sell you on the lie that I have bred
a perennial that has as much pizzazz as
a cheap and trinkety annual. It will come
back every year from its drowsing trips
to hibernation or Spain full of green pretense,
half convincing you it wants to be a friend
when all it wants is to get you, hot and fertile,
into its perennial bed. Love is a poet's old
and well-worn returning trope, its greenery
and its grace, and when you step back to see
if water has begun to up-rush the slender stems
of your child by Reverend Adam Buddle,
I unfold my wings for you and filter sun
upon your face, as if this time I might really
be going, might surely be nearly gone already.
You hold your hand for me to settle on.
Already you are are digging us down,

settling on what roots up the new riches
of our fluttering and sundial days.

XXXIV.

I had planned to get up this morning
and go outside and work in the yard,
to drape my body in a cloak of pine pollen
and move through the multiple saffrons
of dawn.

I won't. I'm tired of my ritual shattering
of leaf beds, the cardinals peering down
at me, a miniature man scratching the land,
shaving it as I do on the morning of funerals,
at dawn.

I want to be a different man, better than
you have seen in recent days, not caring
that the forest tramps slowly toward
our house. I want to read some great poet's
biography, catch a movie, be new words,
in dawn.

I can be what loves us—I know I can,
if I try hard enough. I can be the right kind
of yellow, see myself from higher land.
The trees, when we are not looking,
take one step closer to our house, sing
with dawn.

XXXV.

If I did not need you,
I could see why this dictatorial world
exists, why we must re-witness
the rupture of the thousands' gore
each night on the evening news.

But I need you,
so I can only watch
the forsythia bush in our yard
and wonder when it will blink
into its sun-bright yellows,
guess at whether it most needs
sun or stars
or the closeness of another
when its blossom days
are done.

XXXVI.

I picture Keats as a patient
on Mann's Magic Mountain, coughing
dryly as a summer snowstorm sweeps
poems down toward the sleigh-bell town.

You are the patient sitting on a cold,
flat afternoon-sky couch outside,
and he has been telling you of England
and perhaps, through allusion only,
of Fanny Brawne. You consider speaking
of me and my small achievements,
but you feel yourself falling in love
with John, and I am here to say this:
When another love threatens my
hand reaching toward yours,
go away with it into the falling snow.

I understand. I do. You and John go on
with your walking sticks for exercise
down to the village, throw snowballs
at each other, laugh the rose-blush
on your tubercular cheeks a higher red.
Stop in a café for hot chocolate,
a fluffy croissant, couplets, and intimate
table talk. He will lean forward and speak
to you and say you remind him in many ways
of Fanny, and you will say his poems touch
you in ways no other man ever shall.

I will be in my room in the sanitarium,
asking my attendant not to check on me
this evening. I have never felt the tragedy
of love more keenly than now. And in this
loss my love becomes an opal necklace
you will wear for years as you walk on,
well enough for love, at your new poet's side.

XXXVII.

These flowers are for you,
or rather these words
that represent flowers are for you,
but perhaps you wanted real
blossoms and buds
and would take it badly
if all I could offer were the names
of things I believe would make
you happy. Maybe the problem is
I want my name to make you
happy, my name alone,
not my hand reaching for yours
in the rain, not my eyes, alive
at the story you just told,
but my name alone,
six letters' solitary singing
in their typographical wilderness,
saying: *If you want them,*
they are yours, meaning,
if you want me, call my name.

XXXVIII.

I have decided to let you plow
this year, you, the woman of us,
and already I can see you sitting
high in the tractor's seat, writing
words on our land with the gearshift,
taking hold of my work with ease
as I stand before the woodstove
and wonder how pies assemble
themselves, where reed baskets
grow, and how your hands can be
so lovely when I come in at night.

XXXIX.

I have come to the river
and do not know what I shall do now.
I take your hand and say we'll wade it,
but you point out that it's a mile,
that torrents cracker-off the banks,
crumble them into dessert.

I should have said that
we have come to the river,
but I was afraid. I am afraid
all the time now, of going on living,
of geese flying east for summer,
of my clocks being perfectly in time,
of you going ahead into the water,
heading to the other side
while I wait here and praise
your courage, tell the others
how I could never find out
if god is a god of mercy
or judgment, or if I will cross
without fear when my time comes.

XL.

The tiger swallowtails are back,
and I ask them why, and they say,
"Not to see you, God knows,"
and it's just funny, you know?
They fly oddly, frosting our air
in their layer-cake formations,
yellow-soot, yellow-soot, turning
up in the side yard three days
in a row. "We're back to see *her*,"
they say, hovering around you
as you kneel in the perennial bed
planting a columbine, almost
completely ignoring them.
"We're back because she does
not need us." It is the truth.
Even their wings whisper
your name.

XLI.

I order all the mirrors removed
from the place, even chrome handles
on the stove and fridge, and still I see
my image in your eyes and cannot bear
to be what you show me, even in pity.

Beside the still waters of a pond,
I lean to look and must apologize
to what is refracted there, the face
beneath the prism, still unable
to disfigure numbers, to make your
love for me add up. I can shave by
feel alone, riding the Brailles from here
to Honduras, knowing that the eyes
of everyone we meet sees through
what cannot opaque my sight.

That you care for me still,
that you bear the sugared joints
of my hands with such dignity,
tears at what I take to be the truth
of this world. It makes me wish I might
turn every valley into silvered glass
so that I could see twice what you
claim to see in me, my handsome double
whole again, redeemed by your eyes.

XLII.

We passed the wreck, the woman squatting
in her heavy steps as she bled, and an EMT
leaned by her like an old farmer bent to plow.
Wildflowers in the median nodded bluely,
and sagebrush lay down then rose once more
to bundle in the downslope wind, all razors
made to cut the cloth they tied around her.

You touched my shoulder as you turned,
and I let one eye scan the rear view, said
I hope she was not so seriously hurt,
that he could stop the blood's bright flow.
These days I do not know what you know.
You said nothing, looked into your lap
where hands held themselves for mourning.

Where are the flowers that will lie down
upon our graves? Will they be grown around
here, in China, in a Guatemala hothouse?
I wondered if that injured woman knew
a wilt was in her veins? She might say she
was fine then collapse down to our roots.
I will let nothing harm you. I will leap off

the wilderness of this road before I let you
fall. Let us be bright in the softer briefness.
Let us love before we leave. I want to give
directions you can count on, kneel among
your wreckage, bend to be the sacrifice
for your blossom days. I will watch it grow,
your laughter, brighter than the risen snow.

XLIII.

I wonder what I store
for you inside my
actual body and what
lies in the neural pathways
and so might be
defined as
electrical current
but not an organ
or a bone,
not a thing
but a motion,
and I wonder
if that is what
love is—not you,
not me, but what
lies unseen
and moving between
us, like the Earth
before it is light,
before the sun
arises to sing.

XLIV.

I wonder how deep and how long
my regrets can flourish, if the stall
we felt while flying was just for then
or for all the time we have to come.

I am so sorry. Even if it became mantra
for my sunset days, and I stammered
it a thousand canzones per hour, how
could I reach the full meaning of why
I did so many regrettable things?

The bluejays scream from tree to tree,
and I think it is their snake-cry, warning
you not to trust a man like me, but I
could be wrong—they may just be saying
that in the vinous heart there are streams
too tangled to unknot before the dryness
comes. So I get on with it. I go on with it.

I sit in the window seat and bow down
as the storm breaks inside and out,
as you purify me with your tears,
so much more painful than any hammer,
slammed right upon my sorrowful heart.

XLV.

You do not use your iron
much anymore, so it hibernates
on the shelf in the laundry
room. I am no longer your neat
boy, creases sharp as wit and doubt.

I offer to take down the iron
so you can flatten me out,
but you touch my hand,
say we must go for a walk
now, that I should not
worry so much about things,
the strength of my back,
the rumpling of your heart.

XLVI.

The color of all things changes.
I have gone snow with the summers.
Your maidenhair ferns turn to ash.
And we break out with this love,
in the bright greenery of singing voices,
to accept it all, to mate the harmony
of this blue world until we entwine
and return, love into lovers,
prisms without a need for light.

XLVII.

I want to be subtle now, even elliptical,
so that when I am finished you will not
be sure what I said, much less what I
meant. You will blush, feel that surge
of heaviness in the crotch we all know
but be confused about the chemistry
of it. I don't know what I mean when
I say anything is the point I'm making,
and while I think I may be falling in love
with you, it is possible that peace talks
in Korea may be shining before us all now,
so very near that hope becomes possible,
and I can mask my indifferent reaction
with the color of your gorgeous eyes.

XLVIII.

Your skin, the silvery softness
of my memory of your skin,
and my skin or some substitute
for it, a feel for friction between
our skin or the absence of it,
your eyes in the late-day light,
spring greenery through emeralds,
and my eyes, dark chocolate
and pupils black as a bugless night,
your hands with no rings to say
you are mine or that I have a right to say
anything about the silvery softness
of your skin or the malachite clarity
of your eyes, with which you look
at my skin which is coming toward
your hands, so: see and touch all this
that is yours without a condition,
without the memory of my hands
or the last sound of my shuttered eyes.

XLIX.

I spend the entire date preparing to tell you
that I love you, but first I talk
of atomic weights and measurements
of one part per trillion and how thin
arguments can be and still carry
belief, but proof is the standard,
not belief. And I look at you
and know of no true way
to prove love, that saying it
will be an idea, not a theory,
and so I play with my fork
against the drip of a water glass,
looking for one note you did not
expect to hear, the one I did
not understand how to play
but played beautifully, just the same.

L.

I change us into animals.
We stamp the high fields
looking for better forage,
for sweet water, flowing.
Your muscled steps go
strongly before me,
flanks glistening
with sweat, their richness
smelling of this need
to move and to mate.

We could run forever
if we chose. We could
race down the green
ellipsis, trample each
blade until nothing
is left to cut us.

We come to a glen
and begin to crop
the grass. Your head
rises, and a distant
threat flares nostrils
meant to scent me alone
in this soft green field.

We notice we are
animals. Your whinny
smells of laughter
and fermenting hay bales.
I lean into you
to make sure you
will not think of leaving
me here, just when
I know where we are,
where we are going,
far past the final field.

LI.

I want to light the forest for us
through bioluminescence alone.
We have brought no match to strike
against this summer darkness.

I say there may be a wall of foxfire
unburning the dripline of one spring
that spatters across this wall of stone.
You hold tight to the back of my pants,
fearless, borne of the older night
that brought us to the water's edge.

The darkness grows larger. Cicadas
warn us to stop before the path
runs out. I will not suffer blindness
if you are near me. We will find
our way past what was once darkness
and touch with love when we see it
for the first time, and it shines.

LII.

You misunderstand the pressure of the moon
that I have brought you across the city tonight.

Our flood ripens. Autumn leaves dampen redly
in the park. Across the pond bridge, I halt now,

reluctant to carry the lunar surface on to you,
standing between the twin circles of brightness.

A girl on the bank chunks a rock into the water,
and one moon turns tide, washes toward your

street with waves of oak and smoky sandalwood.
You look out the rain-pebbled window for me,

feel that I have come for you bearing a weight
one man cannot begin to know or misunderstand.

Touch me with the imperatives of seashore, my
shell-bound girl. Scoop me up to your small ear

and listen to the cold distance I will always try
to narrow. I could spread the rain apart for you,

opening its curtains to the impractical moon
I bear for you from bridge to bridge, my bride.

I could see your appled cheeks from here, run
to them for a shine, to sip your new supplication.

But this is not what I meant or why I am standing
on the bridge with these moons. I am here to say

that we are pulled together for all time, to reason
out our arms and eyes, in this last curved surface.

LIII.

I am unbuttoning you, one apology at a time.
I do not hope to see your body or feel the skin
you mostly hide from me. Just yesterday I stood
near a beech tree at our creek and realized
that a lime-green luna month lay spread upon
the bark, as if I had opened the xylem to see
what lives inside that smoothing trunk.

I want to open your chest and see what beats
you into sorrow, to forget if I am looking
at the button or the hole, to know if you
are about to fly away from me, far away,
a migratory missionary bringing the word
from what we were, and loved, to the people.

LIV.

You hang a flower basket
on the front porch,
and within ten minutes
a wren begins to fly in
with bits of nesting material,
shaping her circle, feeling
the weight in her abdomen grow.

I want to break my shell
for you, come out crying
nostrums and pixels,
creating a gentle slope
that from a distance might be
any experience you need.
It sweetens your pain.
It calms the remembered ache
in your breasts. It tumbles
like a child who cannot
be hurt very much in falling.

I will be riding from the shell
with a song for you, wondering
if our touch is the meaning
of sanctuary, and if your wings
as you settle on me from the sky
bring more of our nest to us,
not safety or the absence
of fear but something full
and strong, with new lift
that bears us upward,
high enough to see
other baskets that may bear
the sanctuary of all flowers.

LV.

Our old deaf beagle
does not stir when I leap
up at a golf shot or touchdown
or to rail at some senator
and his rough-bark tongue.
She twitches through it
and might see my mouth
move and wonder if my dance
has any meaning, but she
does not fear for me, has not
been afraid herself for years.
When she sleeps, she hears
nothing. When she awakens,
she stretches in the silence,
wagging her old dog's smile.

When I can no longer hear,
I am trying to say, take my
hand as I stop to look
back and forth in terror
at a corner, not knowing when
to cross, and say to me,
Everything will be all right.

I will see your words
and feel a warm bath of joy
that you are there to call me,
to pet me into silence,
and call me, call me home.

LVI.

Is it our imagination
or do the pastures now bear
a population of goats
that would have seemed
improbable ten years ago?

We do not know one breed
from another, but we know
a goat when it bends to crop
the grass, leans back up,
odd eyes wondering why
we stand on our hind legs
against the fence, faces
crushed, horns lopped,
bleating with odd syllables.

You are my herd, my body,
my fear of storms and howls
of threat or from night's pain.
When you head into the barn,
take me with you. Or stay
here with me through the dark
and teach me to lap the salt
of our acreage from the stars.

LVII.

We awaken colt-young, leaping
into our muscles, unable not to run
and buck, shout at the newly risen day,
punch out its adolescent lights.
How could this have happened?

We are afraid to slow, to ask why
we have begun again, hard bodies,
inconsequential thoughts, no ideas,
really, but bodies and this motion.

The lovely, untimed penetration
of things begins, too, slick streams
of sweat and our chorus-laughter.
We ride on a stallion flash of air,
you behind me, strong arms wrapped
on my chest, all too hard to fall
beneath this improbable youth.

We awaken. O dear God you were
so beautiful as I never was, even
back then, and now we sit on
this Earth and plant gerbera daisies,
perennials, reseeding annuals,
and when I reach for the rake
to lever myself upright, you
look away, not seeing when
I fall, wondering if I have run off
like a mad boy, scorching into awe
the flight path of our first love.

LVIII.

Surely comets make the sound of swans
as they slice above the hills of France.

Surely snow-cone peaks in the Rockies
smell like vanilla as they whiten more.

Surely rivers taste of cinnamon and ice
as they refuse to reach an indifferent sea.

Surely you hear the key in our front door
as I return from my trip, and stand and turn
toward me, jeweled from the darkest sky.

Surely we make the sound of swans
as we rise, apart from the risen world.

LIX.

You are like the rain. Wait, that's me.
I am like the rain, sheeting forests,
steaming up windows, articulating fog
like ornaments in a Bach keyboard piece.

You say, You haven't put an animal
in this poem yet or a color or a fruit,
and so I have to say I'm worried about you,
but don't be, because I am like the rain.

I have no place to go but down,
and with that, I have made my peace.

LX.

If I have a stroke and no longer seem
to know who you are, I will know you.

Trust this, if you trust any place I walk,
anything I say, the singing in my hands.

If I grow mute and half blind, buoyed
by the touch on my touchless side,
I will feel us twenty once more, trembling
with one unknowable need, hitching
myself to you for our spring plowing.

As injured animals try to keep on running
when they lie upon the stricken ground,
I will drop our wooden bucket down
and down farther into the dark coldness
of water. You must not believe in me
as a man who has learned to breathe
that stream so far beneath. I will know
you entirely, run our righteous field
with the bilateral symmetry of love.

You will say, "My God! My God! He is
rising from the bed without a hand,
extending his boy's legs for a run
from here to the rocky mouth of sound!"

The others will forgive you, know
that what is literal cannot continue
those charms. We all come to this numb
conclusion, halfway or with the thorough
joy of loosening, of rapturing our wings
higher than the body we cannot feel.

I am still in here, I will not need to say,
and I am swimming toward us, back
to the penitent green of a newer grace.

LXI.

I wear the wound of you
into broad daylit celebrations,
witness to the sounds
I made you sound out
in the room's heart darkness.

I will not wind a muffler
round my sutured smile
to keep it from the crowd.
They can feel the lift
in my step, the new ruin
of my once enjoyable
self-absorption, but now
I want to wear the wound
of you into the world,
invite believers to dip
their hands into the blood
of our midnight theatrical.

Your smile will tell them
to recall their own rapture,
when they spoke sentences
without speaking, told tales
of themselves as our heroes,
awoke into sunlit disbelief,
and rose to walk the Earth.

LXII.

I am not standing beside the lighthouse
on St. Simon's Island thinking of you,
the way your eyes turn out to sea, bright
enough for all vessels to steer on home.

But I might be, could transport myself
there with potions and spectacular charms,
drape my epiphitic self upon your arms
and begin to rotate in the warm salt breeze.

Tell me if I must. Speak to me with the firm
stones of the firmament, and I will read your
small ship's rudder right into my arms.
We live in the wide glass of our lighthouse,
still alive enough to live our magnifying days,
and when the endings come, I know you
are turning back toward me and will arrive
once more in our schedule, no need to rush
what has been inevitable between us,
each of us guiding the other back where
the length of our beams gleam into joy.

I am not near the lighthouse, but perhaps
I am, for I cannot step outside your glow
here on St. Simon's Island, where each
of us leaves the lights on, long after
the other is long home or long gone on.

LXIII.

It always seemed cool in the summers
when we took a picnic to the fish hatchery
at Walhalla, years before I saw your fins
spread before me in the liquid of all air.

Spruce trees hung over the carved table
at which we sat, my mother spreading
her blessing into our small folded hands.

I worried for the trout in their prison pens,
soon to be released into the fishing streams
where fat men cast on them their spells
to die. But one did not speak of such things,
nor did he speak of where the placid cattle
in their barbed confinement along dirt roads
would one day ride. I had held hands by then
with a girl in our small town's movie house
and wondered if I would ever head out
to sea and find you, if you lived in your fins
and had escaped the streams that other men
had built for you. Once I felt as if I must shout
out a race through the spruce trees, run away
from what held us to the table in deeper shade
than I knew back home. But I never could.

We will all untie our bindings, my grown love,
and break out, break on from the navigation
that we misunderstood, buoyed downstream
by the righteousness of the minnow moon.

LXIV.

The sweetness of well-water is not
what I meant. I was speaking of hands,
how they dip down into morning sinks
with fingers slightly apart, as if cupping
up a clear liquid could not be their role
in this life. I find you hard to explain.

Mirrors are the shrill enemy rising
from the cities of the plain, shrieking
what cannot be the truth of it all.
This is too dramatic. What I am trying
to say is that we live on our old well
quite happily, five hundred and twenty
feet deep and still excited by the draw
spouting from our spigots to see who
shall next feel the wetness we need
to keep this thing going, for the heart
of reproducible nights in which pain
erodes upon a storm of denser delight.

As if I were about to cry out and then
said nothing, making a small drama
speak to us. This is not too dramatic.
I am shaving when you walk behind
me headed for the kitchen, swimming
through the silvered kelp of our glass.

LXV.

I want to find some way to steal your cup
after we have met for coffee, to sit still
in some lost place and lick off the words
you laughed at me. Something of you
lingers in each rub, the desk corner
you touch, the water-cooler's white knob.

Your words vibrate the inner genitalia
of my ears, crisp verbs, unexpected nouns.
We are still sitting at the table, and I know
you will throw the cup in the trash bin,
but I want the warmth of your fingers
in their long lingering around this
paper circle, as you finish a sentence
while lifting it to your fullest lips.

There's Elvis! I could cry, pointing,
but that's a dodge you've heard before,
a man imagining the silk of your eyes
from a different angle, one gift or gifts
that you unknowingly share packed
by him for his secret place, to take
even the smallest part of you to taste.

LXVI.

How can you love me and non-objective art
at the same time, you ask. I see your shapes,
objects bent into color and the possibility
of form, but you need the more-specific
illustrative oaken buckets that Andrew Wyeth
might have painted with egg tempera
on a softened, windy day in your memory.

We do not see our minutes the same way.
I love an order buried deeply in disorder,
so sunken that the *Alvin* would crack apart
trying to retrieve it from the pit of my sight.
You demand the comfort of what is direct
and literal, and so when we see an exhibition
of abstract expressionism you cringe and flee

while I fall myself into the deliciously fractal
funnels thrown down upon the canvas like
a challenge for a child. Also, you do not enjoy
"sad endings" or anything that makes you fear
our common heaven more than you do already.
Love me anyway. Show me the pirate in the picture.
I will show you how beautiful it is to suffer so.

LXVII.

Take off your glasses to carve away
the years from my glance. Who is this
young man who follows you along
the ambivalence of sidewalks, who hums
the hit tune of your small warm hands?

We are past our photorealist days.
From across the gallery, down the street,
we are the movie stars that seekers meet
in delighted dreams. We turn perfect,
caressed by all light, even loved by air.

I feel as if my feet have found their dance,
a tiptoe past sharp focal planes. And color
in my arms for you takes its sudden turn
from arch to arch above on hidden bowers.
This boy smiles into his gift to you: flowers.

LXVIII.

It is raining in this poem.
Weather makes it easier to say goodbye
or hello for the first time, to fold
into a rock shelter and turn to look
at each other with such sober clarity
that falling in love is the only thing
it could be.

Any thunder is far away.
Your hair drips in damp strands, smells
of the rain's cool felicity, and your hands
reach for a long lock and squeeze out
the rain as a cure for recklessness.
I think: Falling in love is the only thing
it could be.

I intend to make it rain
until the end of this poem, harder now,
so thick I must see water in your eyes
through mine, meaning clarity is relative
when showers flow through a story
or a poem. Falling in love is the only thing
it could be.

LXIX.

Our grandson sits
in the inflatable float
that drifts with
your breath
in Wildcat Creek,
and I can see
from his eyes that
he does not want
to sail toward Morocco,
whack sharks
with his tiny cup,
but if it must be so,
he trusts your
breath to keep
him above the pain
of this world.
He knows that if
he takes out the plug
your breath will
make it all right,
say to him *Elliott,*
Elliott, and he could
drift around the
world and return
to our creek whole,
to the place where
fear is no match
for the sound
of you whispering
his much-loved
little name.

LXX.

Can you ever forgive me?
The anthracite heart I showed you,
the veins that roadmap my hands
toward the wrong location of our love?
Can you? I am a weak man,
and for some reason I thought
you would find that attractive,
but this is not the first illusion
I have pulled on myself,
the first tricked-out sleight
of heart in which you did not believe.

I do not know what to think
of a weak man who thought
he could make being a weak man
attractive to a stronger woman.

I do not understand the magic
of allusion anymore, that you
would laugh when I saw myself
in half for you instead of weep,
because I meant for it to hurt,
and when I can no longer hurt
you, I must absolve you
and ask that you see me as
a weak man who might
nevertheless walk toward you
through the densest flames,
who might even walk on water.

LXXI.

The wild onion out by the propane tank
just goes on growing. I think I'll go out
there and find it slumped over, gone gray,
but it seems destined for French cooking,
for a hamburger bulb, slab onto slab.

Interesting. I was going to pull it up
and take it to the farmer's market,
but they will not accept the wildly grown,
the untended, the improbably vegetative
kingdom around us. They want to know
that someone has loved it to maturity,
mothered every tendril with care,
but I prefer my onions wild, the way you
turned on me the first time we met,
and I knew I liked it better this way.

LXXII.

This is the day I will finally
stop talking of you to complete strangers,
I think, but an elderly man is shuffling
along this sidewalk like an antique plane
that means to crash into me if it can,
and I throttle-back and smile on him.

She is my witness and my shade,
I whisper, and he nods, knowing how
a man can falter when she walks
into a room, mismate his steps
with the indifferent floorboards.

He says, She was my heart-pine
and my resurrection. We look down,
not knowing what to say next,
so I do not tell him that you ring
the bells across our continent,
rush rivers through their gorges
with the old chorus of joyfulness.
I do not tell him how your hands
heal the cuts I bear, change me
into a flight of wit and wonder,
warm confessions from my night.

He does not say she changed him
from enigma into rose, lit up his days
too bright for one more thing to die.
He catches what you are in my sigh.
And we pass apart in this our day
of your invocation, and we both go
on to speak, to sing of your arms
and what saves this raptured world.

LXXIII.

What is yet another luna moth
on the window screen in my study
waiting for, anyway? She has spread
herself for display, unpinned
but motionless, probably dead.

I sit and watch for a long time.
I want to see a vague motion,
a spasm of wingbeat as it lifts
her toward a safer distance.

You come into the room and see
me frozen in my chair, looking
pensively out the window
and wonder if I am dead,
if this is how the slow end
of all life begins, lime green
and falling, fiery, to the Earth.
I hush you without turning.

This is worth seeing, I say,
another use for wings,
the beauty of frail things
in a late day's sunlight.

LXXIV.

Tangerine: orange with an attitude.
Lime: lemon with a head-cold.
We walk into the orchard or grove,
the vineyard or cloddy farm field,
without purpose, with our tart times
behind us as lovers, acidic days
rising too often now. We are more like
grapefruit, I fear, bulging, indistinct,
landing with a thud when rolled
off the table of our lives. I don't mind.

Any number of plants taste of sugar
when chewed, like the ribbon cane
my brother and I gnawed as boys.
Things that should be sweet turn
implacably sour on the younger tongue.

I reach up and pick the next ripe fruit
as my gift to you, not knowing its color
or texture, ripeness or ritual tales.
At the age when any present must be
enough, we sit and open its skin
and ours and see the glistening beads
of pomegranate and our bodies' promises
through the settling sun. You brighten
and turn impossibly ripe once more,
and I reach out to pluck you off
before the last leaf lifts, or falls.

LXXV.

How can we know two weeks
before the day we will die?
Is there some large X engraved
on our kitchen calendar, a note
taped to the stove's white door?

I will not go without you.
I will have pulled you into my arms
with more passion than you have
seen in years. You will look at me
the way we did at the young cusp
of this long contagious life's time.

I will say, It's time for you to float
across the world without what
I grieve to give you no longer.
And you will. And in my absence
you will put up a new calendar
on the wall, its X-less leaves
untorn, and in the mirrors
around our house you will see
my shadow as it fades, and you
are strong to mark the days
alone, my shadow gone on
to where you can come later
if you wish, if you feel you must.

LXXVI.

Men have begun to leave off belts
as they did hats in my father's day,
shirt-tails out as the proper casual
attire or even worker's daily dress.

I can't even find my belt for funerals
or weddings—it has burrowed deep
down in the closet for the long sleep
of widows and the quiet unnecessary.

You held me taut in our upright days,
leaned me tall into another drunken
corner, laughed at my leaning jokes.
Now you gather me like the drooping

shock of wheat I am, prop me in the sun
to season as we go on reasoning,
the binding of what ripened long ago
and still holds himself up to you.

LXXVII.

Buckshot holes through the tin walls
of my mechanic's garage, and spread
along the concrete floor, freckles of light,
a boy's summer face, hat lost three days
now and headed for the pond, for bream.

I know less about cars than I have led
you to believe, differential of my life.
I was ashamed not to be your distributor,
to know your firing sequence by heart,
top to bottom, plug by sparking plug.

My mechanic says if it was him, he
would not worry. He knows less of cars
than his wife thinks, too. He says all men
know less than their women had hoped
at one point, but if they fire up now and then

it is enough it is enough it is enough
to go from here to California and back.

LXXVIII.

Touch me the way you touched me
when what was new to us would be new
for its first and only time. I am failing.

We can pretend the new world began
with us, giddy on our arrival, explosive
with need to shower us, shiver us golden.

Maybe I'm not quite failing, but it feels
as if I am, bending bones, an abrupt
weakness of muscles and of all will.

Your hand was coming toward my own
as if possessed by more than its body outright,
an intent, a genuflection of every sunrise.

Your body leaned into mine as we lay
upon the stiffening bed. And your touch
was in the way you looked at our touch.

I can still lean into a wall of nouns and verbs
to hold me up and still. The new world
lights up to see us young and filling here,

again, your soft fingers come to mine mine.

LXXIX.

Walking beneath the canopy
of white oaks and looking up,
I wonder what is hiking over
the canopy of white oaks and
looking down, and if we see in
each other something upside down
or right side up, or if we can
simply not judge what we see,
the way the world judges
right from wrong, high
from low, you from me.

LXXX.

The world's smallest fish swims
in an acidic peat swamp in Indonesia,
7.9 millimeters long, without bones,
trending toward invisibility.

I am that small or much smaller to Earth
in her blue wholeness, and my life
is roughly the same length, so why
do I also live in acid, rub my hands raw
wringing them to turn your fins to me and swim?

There is an apt pointlessness
to all things and a portal for meaning
that might at first seem made for another
function entirely. Which is another way
of saying I have survived this upstream
route for you all the years of my body,
so ridiculously small that you could miss
my unheroic persistence as you float off
toward a jewel of sunbeam on the creek.

It is so hard for me to ask to be loved.
I would be a terrible politician. My scales
fall away like an amp of snow, and I am
laid bare for currents to flow apart.

Yet here I am trying to make myself seen,
to turn your glistening body back
at the most important second of my life
and come with me on the tiny journey
of this microscopic life we must swim.

LXXXI.

Our neighbor is doing something over there
with a front-end loader and a plow.

I can't see the operation entirely, as trees
make mosaics between us, separate scenes
we cannot add into a Currier & Ives house
where children ache-up a Christmas tree
strung with planets in reflected lights.

He could be doing anything, a garden,
planting grass, straightening the driveway.
I could imagine him digging deep down
for a swimming pool, shattering gneiss,
filling the hillslope with bluest shimmers.

I cannot see you this morning. Have you
gone out to change our yard with music
or mourning, to sing up a mockingbird
who knows the secrets of our landscape?

I am your witless designer, the one who
would break your beauty into a world
beyond us. I would remake the Earth
into your image, even if I was the only one
on this Earth who could grow your name.

LXXXII.

Let's be owls, then,
great horns outflanking
sound and warm air,
silent hunting
into the downdrafts.
I want you to see
the kindness in how
I go about my kill
and what then will
take my feathers
off for pillow dreams.

You are the barred owl
that cries beyond
the flood-plain by
the creek, present and
invisible, a brown
circling through
the undercanopy
raking my names
one letter at a time
through the sodden
summer night air.

We who mate
for life can take
so much suffering
that when air lifts
us up into geography
it comes as a delight,
the surprise that
love became when
it first swept us up
and far off our feet.

LXXXIII.

Tin roof there in Mountain City
with the rain spelling our names
in code, an all-day event, and
at night in our cheaply bought
bed, holding on to each other
as any future went far away.

I do not mind my body's breaking.
I do not miss the snaky grass
we let grow to the porch.
I cannot say I miss the ache
I felt when the poor family
up the hill, the one whose horse
we fed apples to, wept as we
spoke our final goodbye.

I miss the rain knowing
the young and younger words
above us to keep us safe
in our own poverty, spelling
the names we choose to bear
and that of the black cat
asleep on your small feet.

LXXXIV.

I am at the stop sign
where Oliver Bridge Road meets
Flat Rock Road, and a yellow school bus,
which has beat me to the intersection
turns with a groan, and sunlight shouts
off the windows, turning them blank,
Little Orphan Annie's eyes. Then
one slight angle lets light out from
inside, and there I am, fourteen,
thinking of Wagner and Bruckner,
skin stuck to the seat as I jostle
in a Mendelssohnian rhythm,
wonder what I could become.

We are always checking evolution
in the mirror, the clear counterpoint
of age spots, the motif of hair and hands.
I have realized for years that I am not
desirable anymore, not to you or anyone
else on the bus, that my Rhine Journey
is from one room to another around
the house. I am waiting to go,
but the stop sign cannot relent
at this point, and so I lie back
among the French horns and listen.

Did I ever catch you looking at me
with your shy smile, your thick satchel?
We were going the same way, I want
to believe, to school or home from it.
The glare on the windows showed me
Bach: passions, partitas, and gigues.

I was at the stop sign
and did not know it, then you came
across the aisle toward me and moved
as we sang our lives, and you forgave me

for never being famous, for trying
to compose myself better in the ecstasy
of your unexpected closeness.

LXXXV.

Let's look forward
to senility equally,
silver shimmering,
ivory grown agleam.

We could fall in love
again when we do
not know the other's
name, set up a date
in the formal garden
of our rest home,
have May Chapman
for our chaperone,
she, the humorless
former librarian
in Bungalow 2-B.

You can reconfigure
my bow-tie for me,
and I will go find
for you a matching
sock. We will dance
in the cool gazebo,
step across our
last lives with slow
and purposeful steps.

I have been looking
so forward to this,
I will tell you,
waltz, fox-trot,
and taking all the time
left in this world
to learn your name.

LXXXVI.

Perhaps it would have been better
if we had stayed strangers, one old man
shouldering into you as he bought canvases,
and you looked for grandkid watercolors.

You would turn once to me, step aside,
hum up excuses to remain untouched.
I would try on a noncommittal smile
and nod as if we had met so long ago

that neither of us could then remember.
Then we would begin to know the years
we spent together, the mountain trips,
the bending back into cold waterfalls

on the road from Highlands to Franklin.
Maybe it would be better if I had not
run into this strangeness, our acrylic
images as they paint themselves again

from aisle to aisle. But it happened,
and as I came around erasers blanking
out all memory, you were there before
me, and we puzzled: Where did I see

you in the past, and where did we go
when the years poured down their tides
upon us? You guess the same tale I do.
We have spent this life together, hear

ourselves cry for witnesses in the wild,
one of us the parent, the other one the child.

LXXXVII.

I have been wanting you
to touch me
for the longest time,
longer than it takes
limestone to drip
a cavern full of teeth
meant to tear
nothing, gentle
incisors made
to mediate speech
of a singular kind.

Just come up
beside me
and put your hand
on my shoulder
but lightly so
I cannot know
if you wish me
to turn or just
want me to know
you are here,
dripping down
from the ceiling
of this need
and slowly making
me go ahead
and rise.

LXXXVIII.

Some grave battle must have turned
the course of history on this date
but I don't care about that now. I am
thinking of rain, of signs the squirrels
might make to each other to beckon
or warn off their closest friends,
to imply an intimate moment between
or beyond them. And if we have been
at war with each other this week,
here is my sign, my cache for winter,
the scrape of my fur on our branch,
the promise that binds us together
in the green world, the high nest,
the cautious chattering of dawn.

LXXXIX.

I want to make sense when I am around you.
I want to be properly groomed. I want to hum
if you like humming—I inferred this from a comment
you made about hummingbirds, but maybe I was wrong.

I want to sit up straight. I want to make you feel smarter
than I am by complimenting, but not too much, the things
you say. I want to laugh at anything you tell that might
be a joke, even if I'm not sure you meant it as a joke.

I want to compliment the colors you love most, alone
or in combinations, find out your favorite movies
and invent anecdotes about how I felt when I first saw
them. I want to know your politics better, so I can
look up some obscure fact and say it as an afterthought,
that Millard Filmore had no vice president because
he became chief executive when Zachary Taylor died,
that kind of thing. I want to compliment your eyes.

I will say you have the hands of Diana, mistress
of the hunt, strong enough to bend back a bow.
I want to invent a plausible life of my own that you
can find yourself liking, effectively hide the real me,
which I can't imagine you liking much or thinking of
when you are just sitting on the porch and humming.

XC

I am not strong.
You will have to be
the first one whose memory
goes. Otherwise you will
know as the years pass
that I am not the one
you should turn to
when night comes
and a thousand
sounds break the glass
of silence in the dark woods
beyond the edge
of our property, at the place
where someone else might
live, where there are powers
we cannot control,
where the light ends,
and beyond which
there be dragons.

XCI.

Jump off the diving board,
you in your nine-year-old's
swimsuit, no need to shave
or feel self-conscious yet
about the new awkwardness
of your body. Almost nothing
holds the top up. You play
with the straps like a kitten
slaps a skein of blue string.

I wish I had known you then,
when you gangled off the side
of the pool like a spider leaping
into the heart of its feeding net.
You had no presuppositions,
no need for a boy's rough hand
on your shoulder, the new low
vowels of a kid whose voice
had just begun to break itself
on the promises of your eyes.

We would dive down deeper,
to the penny-grabbing bottom
of the pool, and open our eyes
to see each other. And I would
think I saw something in how
you smiled at me, some promise
for the later life that we could
never find again in our thin-clad
bodies, our watery younger selves.

XCII.

I bought you a river
for our anniversary, and they
are delivering it Tuesday.
At first I was undecided
between the Orinoco
and the Danube, but finally,
to show you the long flow
of my affection and years,
I ordered the Nile,
but without crocodiles
and poisonous snakes,
generally stocked with otters
and penguins and harp seals,
soft witnesses to the day
on which we joined hands
and began to flow toward
the sea as we understood it,
a life without borders,
and deeper than the stars.

XCIII.

When they announce the end of the world,
I am hoping we do not have months, years,
but maybe fifteen minutes, enough time
to make our quick goodbyes. I want to know
you believed in me. I need to see your hand
wrangling mine as we snuggle into *gone*.

Why, I say, stroking your hair, it's just like
any death, the world around us growing quiet,
our time slowing to a storyteller's final words.

We will not speak of meaning. At the end,
meaning means nothing, and you will hum
a song your grandmother knew, as I speak
your name over and over. In the distance
it will begin to roar toward us, but I will
say, Let it be the sound of ocean waves
breaking into a beach's cracked shell-bed.

Curlews will cry for the sight of small fish,
diving down into their dying days, the pain
slighter than shadows of sea oats by morning
light. And you will swim with me out to sea
in the heat of our memorial blood. The sky
explodes in a terminal smile upon us both.

We are being loved as our hearts take us down.

XCIV.

We have not yet decided
if we shall be buried or burned,
struck in stone or just a song
whose tune stays clear
to our grands and greats
while only fragments of our
lyrics remain. We can wait,
I think, hold off on furnaces
or die-cut lettering for a while
at least. I want to watch golf
today, doze through a Braves
game, not decide anything
of importance. My grandfather,
gone for thirty-three years
would lie in the dark listening
to the Cardinals on the radio
late in his life, and I am sure
he had not picked the blue suit
in which we would bury him,
in which he still lies, now
in the baseball season, beneath
a stone, up in South Carolina.

XCV.

There are hundreds of websites
with ways to kill wild grape vines,
but what if one loves their sway
in an autumn breeze? I cannot find
a site that tells me how to look
at them as one listens to
Music for St. James the Great
by Guillaume Dufay, as one might
more closely examine Ghiberti's
Gates of Paradise, the way you
can stand in midtown Manhattan
just before dawn and hear so little
that you swear this girl's glance
from last week is a prelude to love.

I feel her growing greenly into me.
I want to be entwined, knotted up
with her, with you, I mean, since
third-person cannot live long
when love comes, just as these
climbing lianas of wild grape vines
will die back when cold weather
comes, having reached their peak
and seen through the old canopy
that there is light. It all turns light.

XCVI.

I'll come back.
I'll probably come back
soon is what I mean.

I'll return with
a basket of tomatoes
still warm from sun
and my hands.

You can quarter them
for a salad when
I come back,
and we can sit
beneath the arbor
and eat our salads when
the sun comes out,
if it ever does again,
when I come back,
if I do, and I will,
and instead of tomatoes

I may just give you
the sun to hold snug
against you on
a cold winter night,
or you can hold me.

It's your choice.
It always has been.

XCVII.

Loud storm over us:
oil lamps and candles,
the aroma of matches
and the soggy shifting
of wicks: you by pale
flames trying to read
and me taking stock
of the trees falling
around us that say
cut me, carve me,
burn me, use me
to ruin the night
of its old blackness.

XCVIII.

The pay phones have
paid off their final debts
and retired to Florida,
I suppose. They must
hang out in the cradles
where they napped away
their ringing years. No
one calls them anymore.

Sometimes they must turn
and think that surely they
have heard the sound of bells
from another nearby room.

They do not let a lover
weep from New Jersey
to Las Vegas now, cannot
translate the giddy joyfulness
of a girl glowing in her smile.

No one puts in another
quarter, begs a passerby
frantically for a coin to keep
a father on the fading line.

Am I this useless to you
now that we have grown old
together? I want to awaken
you with my familiar ringing,
the tone of our kisses in the dark,
the insistent code of bells
calling out my private name
for you alone, for you always,
from here to the last number
on the sun's enduring dial.

XCIX.

That was the year the morning glories
bloomed unexpectedly, frost just gone
beyond our neighbor's hill. And you asked
me, as I left, to buy fresh bread when
I came home, and I said, I surely will.
The wheat was green as gravegrass
upwind on old Taggart's road. A combine
stood undriven for a season or more.
And in that yeasty photograph, I imagined
that the grain was not asleep but rising
in the lovely ovens, hot as August, ready
for the staleness that will break our bones.
You stood by the morning glories, waving
as I drove away, not saying what we say
to make our love rise each old day,
answering with your eyes
what I meant to ask and then forgot.
You said, *I will*, as the blossoms curled
and loved along the sunstroked sill.
You said, *I surely will.*